W9-BHY-968

From Your Friends at The MAILBOX®

Clarification

Writing

Grades 4–6

Project Manager:
Kim T. Griswell

Writer:
Pat Twohey

Contributing Editors:
Cayce Guiliano, Liz Lindsay, Scott Lyons, Thad H. McLaurin,
Jennifer Munnerlyn

Art Coordinator:
Clevell Harris

Artists:
Pam Crane, Teresa R. Davidson, Nick Greenwood, Clevell Harris,
Greg D. Rieves, Barry Slate, Donna K. Teal

Cover Artists:
Nick Greenwood and Kimberly Richard

Writing Works!

www.themailbox.com

Manufactured in the United States

10 9 8 7 6 5 4 3 2

Table of Contents

About This Book

What Is Clarification Writing?

In *clarification writing,* a writer states whether she likes or dislikes something. The writer then supports her reasoning with three or more specific details and summarizes her opinion in a concluding sentence.

Develop and enhance your students' clarification-writing skills with this easy-to-use collection of 20 two-page lessons. *Writing Works!—Clarification* contains everything you need to supplement a successful writing program in your classroom.

Each two-page lesson contains the following:
- A motivating writing prompt
- Simple steps for teaching the prewriting and writing stages of each lesson
- A student reproducible that is either a graphic organizer used in the prewriting stages or a pattern on which students write their final drafts
- Suggestions for publishing or displaying students' work

Also included:
- A reproducible proofreading checklist for the student
- A reproducible clarification-writing assessment for the teacher
- 16 extra clarification-writing prompts
- A student reproducible containing 13 commonly used editing symbols

Other books in the Writing Works! series:
- *Writing Works!—Descriptive*
- *Writing Works!—Narrative*
- *Writing Works!—Explanatory*
- *Writing Works!—Persuasive*
- *Writing Works!—Expressive*

Color My World

PROMPT

Colors are all around us and affect every person in interesting and different ways. Think of your favorite color and your least favorite color. In two clarification paragraphs explain why you like your favorite color and why you dislike your least favorite color.

I just love purple! It's my favorite color!

Think It!

1. Display five different-colored sheets of construction paper on the chalkboard. Below each sheet draw two columns labeled "Like" and "Dislike." Ask each student to select the color displayed that she likes the best and the color she likes the least. Give each student two sticky notes. Next, instruct her to write on one note a brief statement explaining why she likes one color. Then have her do the same on the other note, explaining why she dislikes one color. Direct each student to place each note in the appropriate column on the board. Have students share responses, evaluate the data, and draw conclusions based on the responses.

2. Explain to your students that in clarification writing the writer states whether she likes or dislikes something. Further explain that the writer then supports her reasoning with three or more details and summarizes her opinion in a concluding sentence.

3. Read aloud the prompt above, display it on a transparency, or write it on the board. Then give each student one copy of page 5.

4. Direct each student to use page 5 to help her organize her thoughts about why she likes and dislikes each color.

Write It!

1. Have each student use the information recorded on page 5 to help her write, on another sheet of paper, two clarification paragraphs about her favorite and least favorite colors. Instruct the student to state the color she likes at the beginning of the first paragraph and the color she dislikes at the beginning of the second paragraph. Next, have her support each choice with three or more specific details and then summarize each paragraph in a concluding statement.

2. Direct the student to proofread and edit her work carefully. Encourage students to swap papers to peer-edit. After all corrections have been made, have the student write her final copy on another sheet of paper.

3. If desired, have each student make a favorite/least favorite color collage. Supply each student with a large sheet of construction paper, glue, scissors, and old magazines. Instruct the student to cut out several pictures that contain her favorite color and several pictures that contain her least favorite color. Next, have the student arrange and glue the favorite-color pictures into a collage on the left-hand side of the construction paper; then have her repeat the process with the least-favorite-color pictures on the right-hand side of the paper. Display each student's writing and collage on a bulletin board titled "Color Our World."

Color My World

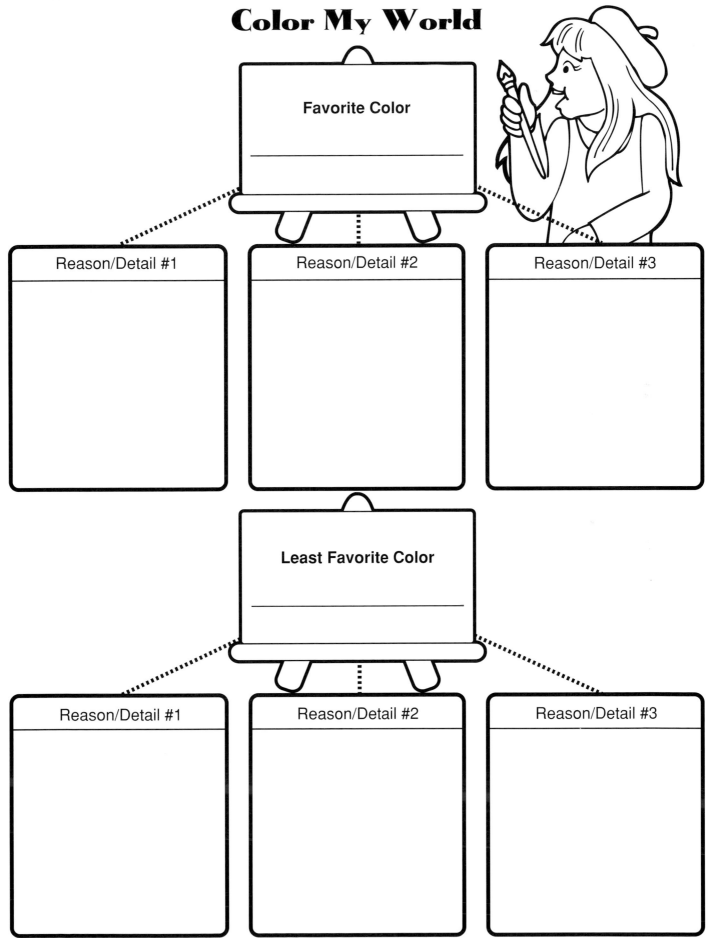

Favorite Color

_____

Reason/Detail #1

Reason/Detail #2

Reason/Detail #3

Least Favorite Color

_____

Reason/Detail #1

Reason/Detail #2

Reason/Detail #3

Long Distance

PROMPT *Communicating with faraway friends is great fun. You can write a letter, send an email, or talk on the phone. Which method do you prefer? Write a clarification paragraph explaining which method of communication you prefer to use and why.*

Think It!

1. Have your students help you list on the board the various ways to communicate with a long-distance friend. Encourage your students to think of standard as well as more creative ways of communication, such as carrier pigeon, hiring a messenger, etc. Next, have students identify the most common modes of long-distance communication used today: telephone, letter, and email.

2. Explain to your students that in clarification writing the writer states whether he likes or dislikes something. Further explain that the writer then supports his reasoning with three or more details, and summarizes his opinion in a concluding sentence.

3. Read aloud the prompt above, display it on a transparency, or write it on the board.

4. Give each student one copy of page 7. Instruct the student to use the top half of page 7 to organize his thoughts for his paragraph.

Write It!

1. Have each student use the information he's recorded on page 7 to help him write on another sheet of paper, his two paragraphs. Remind the student to include a topic sentence that states his opinion, at least three detail sentences that explain his reasoning, and a concluding sentence in each paragraph.

2. Direct each student to proofread and edit his work carefully. Encourage students to swap papers to peer-edit. After all corrections have been made, have the student write his final copy in the space provided at the bottom of page 7.

3. If desired, use the following idea to display your students' final writings. Cover a bulletin board in bright paper. Then divide the board into three columns. Label one column "Telephone," one "Email," and one "Letter." Then have each student post his final writing in the appropriate column. Title the display "Favorite Mode of Communication." After each student has posted his writing, have the class evaluate the results. Did more students prefer one mode of communication over another?

Long Distance

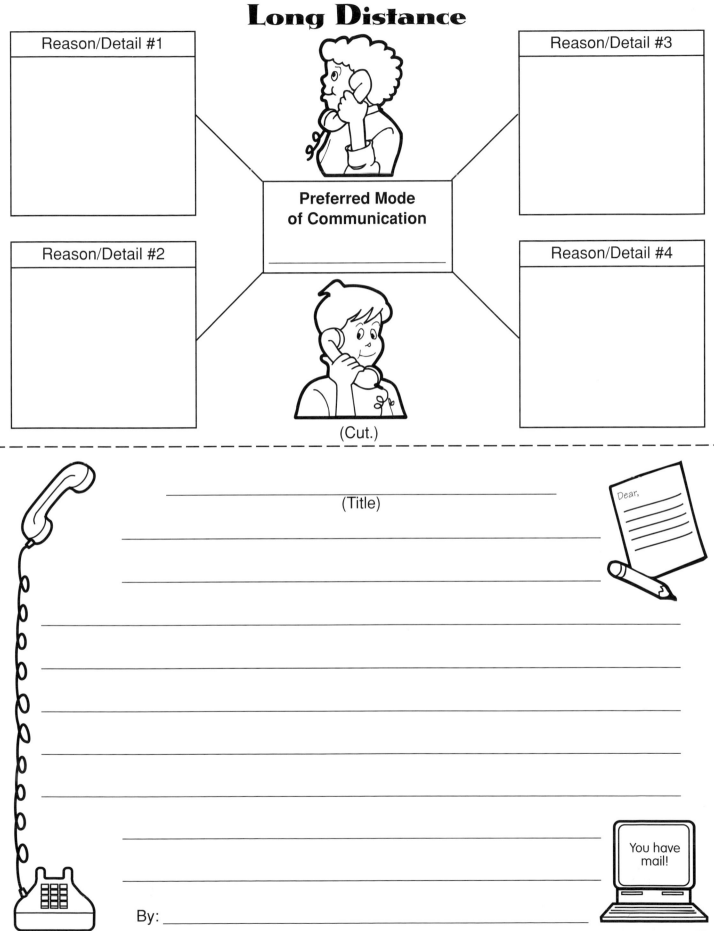

Reason/Detail #1

Reason/Detail #3

Preferred Mode of Communication
_____

Reason/Detail #2

Reason/Detail #4

(Cut.)

_____
(Title)

Dear,

You have mail!

By: _____

Finicky Footwear

PROMPT

From boots to sandals, people like different shoes. Think of your favorite pair of shoes; then write a clarification paragraph explaining why you prefer that particular type of footwear.

Think It!

1. A few days before presenting this lesson, ask several student volunteers to each bring a favorite pair of shoes to class. On the day of the lesson, display the shoes and have the class brainstorm the different characteristics of each type of footwear. (For example: when the shoes are worn, how they feel, how much they cost, etc.) Record their responses on the board.

2. Show students your favorite pair of shoes, and give reasons why you prefer that pair. Tell students that when stating a like or dislike they should be able to provide specific details to support their reasoning.

3. Explain to students that in clarification writing the writer states whether she likes or dislikes something. Further explain that the writer then supports her reasoning with three or more specific details and summarizes her opinion in a concluding sentence.

4. Read aloud the prompt above, display it on a transparency, or write it on the board. Then give each student one copy of page 9.

5. Direct each student to use page 9 to organize her thoughts about her preferred type of footwear.

Write It!

1. Instruct each student to use the information recorded on page 9 to help her write a clarification paragraph about her favorite type of footwear on another sheet of paper. Remind the student to include a topic sentence that states her opinion, at least three detail sentences that explain her reasoning, and a concluding sentence.

2. Direct the student to proofread and edit her work carefully. Encourage students to swap papers to peer-edit. After all corrections have been made, have the student write her final version on a decorated cutout of her favorite type of shoe.

3. If desired, display the cutouts on a bulletin board titled "Finicky Footwear." Or laminate the cutouts and tape them to the classroom floor, creating a path.

Finicky Footwear

Shoes: _____

Topic Sentence: *I like...* _____

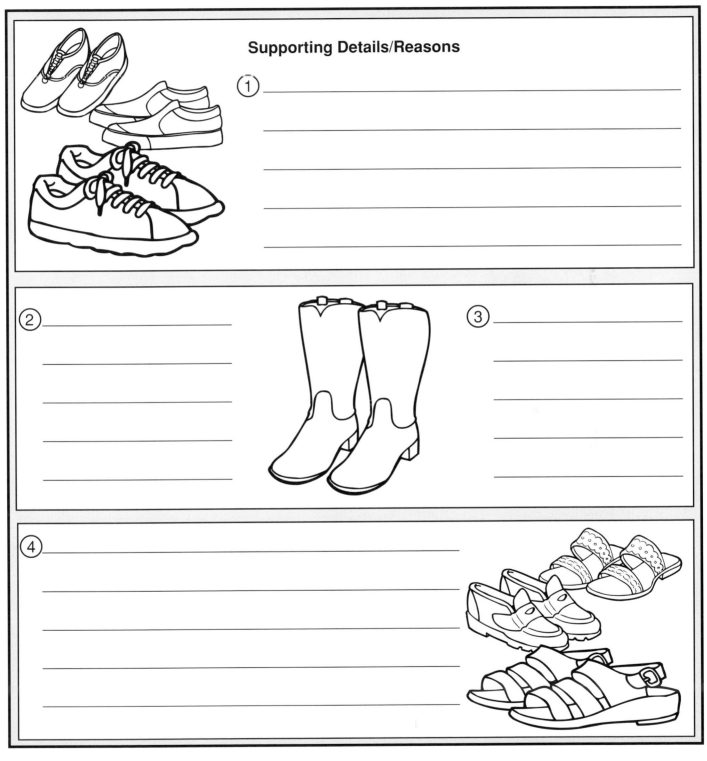

Supporting Details/Reasons

① _____
_____
_____
_____

② _____
_____
_____

③ _____
_____
_____

④ _____
_____
_____
_____

Conclusion: _____

Adventure Travel

PROMPT *Imagine you are a courageous explorer who enjoys activities like climbing Mt. Everest and floating down the Nile River. Write a clarification paragraph telling where you'd like to explore and explaining why you prefer this location.*

Think It!

1. As a class, brainstorm a list of adventure trips (for example: a trip to Antarctica, a trek through a rain forest, etc.). List student responses on the board. Then ask several student volunteers to explain why they would want to take one of the trips on the list.

2. Explain to students that in clarification writing the writer states whether he likes or dislikes something. Further explain that the writer then supports his reasoning with three or more specific details, and summarizes his opinion in a concluding sentence.

3. Read aloud the prompt above, display it on a transparency, or write it on the board. Then give each student one copy of page 11.

4. Direct each student to use page 11 to organize his thoughts about his trip.

Write It!

1. Instruct each student to use the information on page 11 to help him write a clarification paragraph on another sheet of paper. Remind the student to include a topic sentence that states his opinion, at least three details or reasons that explain his reasoning, and a concluding sentence.

2. Direct the student to proofread and edit his work carefully. Encourage students to swap papers to peer-edit. After all corrections have been made, have the student write his final version on a sheet of lined paper.

3. If desired, have each student add two small student-drawn "photos" of the trip below his paragraph. Display the paragraphs and drawings in a photo album titled "Our Amazing Adventures."

Name _____

Adventure Travel

Destination: _____

Topic Sentence: _I think..._ _____

Supporting Details/Reasons

① _I ♡ Rafting_

② PARIS

③ Mt. Everest

④ DIVE

⑤ Surf King

Conclusion: _____

If I Could Pick a Pet...

PROMPT *Imagine you've been asking for a pet for years. Today your parents finally told you that if you chose your favorite pet, they would get it for you. In a clarification paragraph, tell what animal you'd like to have the most as a pet and why.*

Think It!

1. Brainstorm with your students a list of animals that would make good pets. Then brainstorm a second list of all the qualities of a good pet. Have several student volunteers tell what types of pets they have and share with the class some of their pets' good qualities.

2. Explain to your students that in clarification writing the writer states whether she likes or dislikes something. Further explain that the writer then supports her reasoning with three or more details and summarizes her opinion in a concluding sentence.

3. Read aloud the prompt above, display it on a transparency, or write it on the board. Then give each student one copy of page 13.

4. Direct each student to use page 13 to help her organize her thoughts about why her chosen animal is her favorite and why it would make such a good pet for her.

Write It!

1. Have each student use the information recorded on page 13 to help her write a clarification paragraph about her chosen pet on another sheet of paper. Instruct the student to state the animal she likes, explain her choice with three or more specific details, and summarize her paragraph with a concluding sentence.

2. Direct the student to proofread and edit her work carefully. Encourage students to swap papers to peer-edit. After all corrections have been made, have the student write her final copy on another sheet of paper.

3. If desired, have the students cut out pictures of animals from old magazines and work together to create a bulletin board containing mini collages of animals grouped under fish, birds, mammals, and reptiles and amphibians. Then have the students post their finished paragraphs under the appropriate collages. Title the display "If I Could Pick a Pet…"

If I Could Pick a Pet...

(Type of pet)

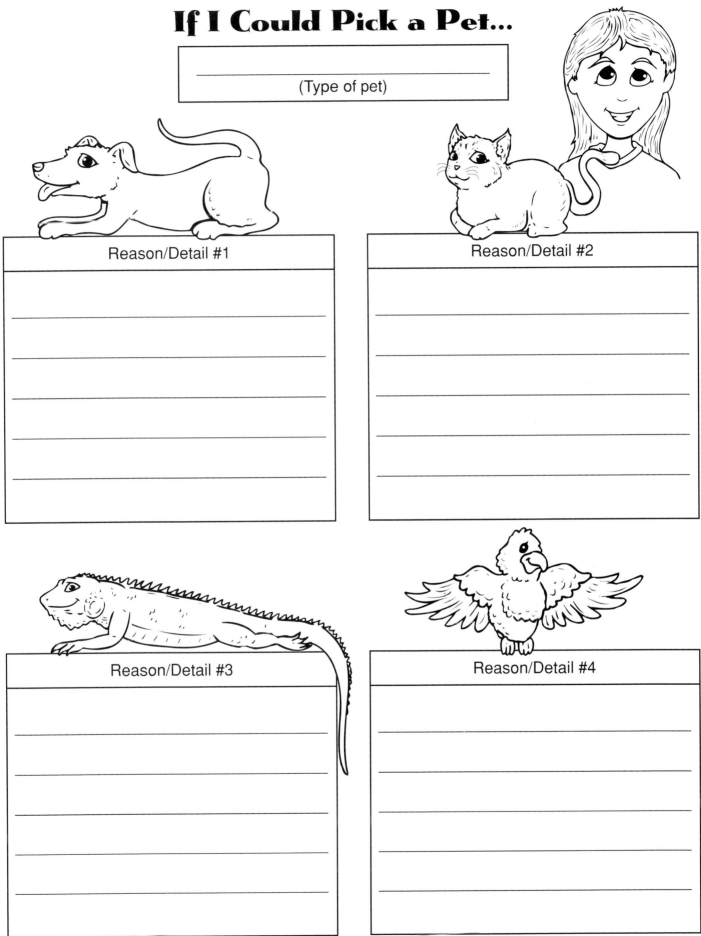

Reason/Detail #1

Reason/Detail #2

Reason/Detail #3

Reason/Detail #4

Guess Who's Coming to Dinner?

PROMPT

The local television station is having a contest and the winner gets to have dinner with his or her favorite celebrity. To enter, all you have to do is write a clarification paragraph telling the name of your special celebrity and explaining why he or she is your favorite.

Think It!

1. Write the word *celebrity* on the board and have a student volunteer read the definition from a dictionary. Discuss the meaning with the class and ask students to think about how someone becomes famous. Then ask students to name celebrities, encouraging them to think of celebrities from different fields (athletes, actors, musicians, etc.).

2. Explain to your students that in clarification writing the writer states whether he likes or dislikes something. Further explain that the writer then supports his reasoning with three or more details and summarizes his opinion in a concluding sentence.

3. Read aloud the prompt above, display it on a transparency, or write it on the board. Then give each student one copy of page 15.

4. Direct each student to use the reproducible to help him organize his thoughts about why he chose the celebrity that he did.

Write It!

1. Have each student use the information recorded on page 15 to help him write a clarification paragraph about his celebrity on another sheet of paper. Instruct the student to name his favorite celebrity, explain his choice with three or more specific details, and summarize his paragraph with a concluding sentence.

2. Direct the student to proofread and edit his work carefully. Encourage students to swap papers to peer-edit. After all corrections have been made, have the student write his final copy on another sheet of paper.

3. If desired, have students draw pictures of their favorite celebrities. Then post each student's illustration and paragraph on a bulletin board titled "Guess Who's Coming to Dinner?"

Clarification writing

Guess Who's Coming to Dinner?

(name of celebrity)

1 Detail/Reason

2 Detail/Reason

3 Detail/Reason

4 Detail/Reason

My Favorite Weather

PROMPT

Rain, snow, hot, or cold—do you have a favorite type of weather? Write a clarification paragraph about your favorite type of weather explaining why it is your favorite.

Think It!

1. Brainstorm with students different types of weather. List their responses on the board. Then divide the class into groups. Challenge each group to list on a sheet of paper the activities they like to do and the different clothes they like to wear in each of the different types of weather listed. For example, under "Rain" a student might list "play in puddles" and "wear boots and a raincoat"; under "Snow" a student might list "build an igloo" and "wear a sweater, coat, boots, and mittens."

2. Explain to your students that in clarification writing the writer states whether she likes or dislikes something. Further explain that the writer then supports her reasoning with three or more details and summarizes her opinion in a concluding sentence.

3. Read aloud the prompt above, display it on a transparency, or write it on the board. Then give each student a copy of page 17.

4. Direct each student to use page 17 to help organize her paragraph, listing details or reasons for why she likes the type of weather she's chosen.

Write It!

1. Have each student use the information recorded on page 17 to help her write a clarification paragraph about her favorite type of weather. Instruct the student to state the type of weather she likes at the beginning of the paragraph. Next, have her support her choice with three or more details and then summarize her paragraph in a concluding sentence.

2. Direct the student to proofread and edit her work carefully. Encourage students to swap papers to peer-edit. After all corrections have been made, have the student write her final copy on another sheet of paper.

3. If desired, give each student a piece of construction paper and instruct her to illustrate her paragraph on one side and glue her final copy on the other side. Then have the student attach a length of string to the top. For a cool 3-D display, hang the illustrated writings from the ceiling.

My Favorite Weather

Reason/Detail #1

Reason/Detail #2

My favorite type of weather is _____.

Reason/Detail #3

Reason/Detail #4

Save Our Planet!

PROMPT *In the news, you often read or hear about ways people are dealing with air, water, noise, and/or land pollution. In two clarification paragraphs, tell what you like and dislike about your school's efforts to help improve the environment.*

Think It!

1. List the four types of pollution (air, water, noise, and land) on the board. Ask student volunteers to share different ways to fight each type of pollution. List their responses under each category.

2. Explain to your students that in clarification writing the writer states whether he likes or dislikes something. Further explain that the writer then supports his reasoning with three or more details and summarizes his opinion in a concluding sentence.

3. Read aloud the prompt above, display it on a transparency, or write it on the board. Then give each student a copy of page 19.

4. Direct the student to use page 19 to organize his thoughts for each paragraph.

CANS   **PAPER**

Write It!

1. Have the student use the information recorded on page 19 to help write, on another sheet of paper, two clarification paragraphs about what he likes and dislikes about his school's efforts to help the environment. Remind the student to include in each paragaph a topic sentence that states his opinion, at least three detail sentences that explain his reasoning, and a concluding sentence.

2. Direct the student to proofread and edit his work carefully. Encourage students to swap papers to peer-edit. After all corrections have been made, have the student write his final copy on another sheet of paper.

3. If desired, give each student a piece of blue construction paper and have him draw and cut out a large earth shape. Then instruct the student to glue his final copy onto the cutout and illustrate the blue border around his final version with details from his writing. Display the final products on a bulletin board titled "Save Our Earth!"

Name _____

Save Our Planet!

What I *like* about my school's efforts to help the environment

Likes:

1. _____

_____

2. _____

_____

3. _____

_____

4. _____

_____

Dislikes:

1. _____

_____

2. _____

_____

3. _____

_____

4. _____

_____

What I *dislike* about my school's efforts to help the environment

Vegetables: Delectable or Detestable?

PROMPT

Have you ever been told to eat your vegetables? Think of your favorite vegetable and your least favorite vegetable. In two clarification paragraphs explain why you like your favorite vegetable and why you dislike your least favorite vegetable.

Think It!

1. Bring to class a variety of vegetables cut into bite-size pieces for your students to sample. Then have students brainstorm a list of vegetables as you record their responses on the board. Give each student a sheet of paper and direct her to divide the vegetables listed on the board into two categories: "Veggies I like" and "Veggies I don't like."

2. Instruct each student to choose one vegetable from each category. Then have her record reasons for liking or disliking each vegetable. Tell students that when stating a like or dislike they should be able to provide specific details to support their reasoning.

3. Explain to students that in clarification writing the writer states whether she likes or dislikes something. Further explain that the writer then supports her reasoning with three or more specific details and summarizes her opinion in a concluding sentence.

4. Read aloud the prompt above, display it on a transparency, or write it on the board. Then give each student one copy of page 21.

5. Direct each student to use page 21 to organize her thoughts about her favorite and least favorite vegetables.

Write It!

1. Instruct each student to use the information recorded on page 21 to help write the two clarification paragraphs on another sheet of paper. Remind the student to include in each paragraph a topic sentence that states her opinion, at least three detail sentences that explain her reasoning, and a concluding sentence.

2. Direct the student to proofread and edit her work carefully. Encourage students to swap papers to peer-edit. After all corrections have been made, have the student write her final version on a sheet of lined paper.

3. If desired, compile the students' papers into one book titled "Vegetables: Delectable or Detestable?" Share the book with a younger grade that is completing a health or science unit on nutrition.

Vegetables: Delectable or Detestable?

Vegetable I like: _____ Vegetable I don't like: _____

Topic Sentence: _____ Topic Sentence: _____

_____ _____

Supporting details/reasons

① _____

② _____

③ _____

④ _____

① _____

② _____

③ _____

④ _____

Conclusion: _____

_____

Conclusion: _____

_____

Free-Time Fun or Folly?

PROMPT

You have the day off and you can do anything you want! Think about your favorite free-time activity and your least favorite free-time activity. In two clarification paragraphs, explain what you like about your favorite activity and what you dislike about your least favorite activity.

Think It!

1. Share with students different activities you like doing and dislike doing in your free time. Ask student volunteers to share activities they like (for example, reading or playing outside) and dislike (for example, cleaning their room or doing yard work). List students' responses on the board.

2. Explain to your students that in clarification writing the writer states whether he likes or dislikes something. Further explain that the writer then supports his reasoning with three or more details and summarizes his opinion in a concluding sentence.

3. Read aloud the prompt above, display it on a transparency, or write it on the board. Then give each student a copy of page 23.

4. Direct the student to use page 23 to help him organize his thoughts for each paragraph.

Write It!

1. Have the student use the information recorded on page 23 to help him write two clarification paragraphs about his favorite and least favorite free-time activities on another sheet of paper. Remind the student to include in each paragraph a topic sentence that states his opinion, at least three detail sentences that explain his reasoning, and a concluding sentence.

2. Direct the student to proofread and edit his work carefully. Encourage students to swap papers to peer-edit. After all corrections have been made, have the student write his final copy on another sheet of paper.

3. If desired, give each student a 9" x 12" sheet of construction paper. Instruct him to fold his paper in half, reopen it, and label one half "Free-Time Likes" and the other half "Free-Time Dislikes." Have the student illustrate each side accordingly and staple his final copy of the paragraphs onto the bottom middle of the illustrated paper. Display on a bulletin board titled "Free-Time Fun or Folly?"

Name _____

Free-Time Fun or Folly?

In my free time I like

Reasons

① _____

② _____

③ _____

In my free time I dislike

Reasons

① _____

② _____

③ _____

Commercial Critics

Television commercials can be informative, funny, boring, or annoying. Think about your favorite and least favorite commercials. In two clarification paragraphs, explain why you like your favorite commercial and why you dislike your least favorite commercial.

Think It!

1. Before teaching this lesson, videotape six appropriate television commercials familiar to students. Show the commercials to the class and ask student volunteers to give their opinions of each commercial. View each commercial a second time, asking each student to analyze what it is that she likes or dislikes about each commercial.

2. Explain to your students that in clarification writing the writer states whether she likes or dislikes something. Further explain that the writer then supports her reasoning with three or more details and summarizes her opinion in a concluding sentence.

3. Read aloud the prompt above, display it on a transparency, or write it on the board. Then give each student a copy of page 25.

4. Direct each student to use page 25 to help organize her thoughts for each paragraph.

Write It!

1. Have each student use the information recorded on page 25 to help write two clarification paragraphs about her favorite and least favorite commercials on another sheet of paper. Remind the student to include in each paragraph a topic sentence that states her opinion, at least three detail sentences that explain her reasoning, and a concluding sentence.

2. Direct the student to proofread and edit her work carefully. Encourage students to swap papers to peer-edit. After all corrections have been made, have the student write her final copy on another sheet of paper.

3. If desired, use the following presentation with your students. Get a large cardboard box, cut a large square hole in one side, and color or decorate the outside to look like a TV. Then have each student present her writing to the class by sitting inside the box while presenting her paper as if she were an actor in a commercial. After students have completed their presentations, display their final copies on a bulletin board titled "Critics' Choice."

Commercial Critics

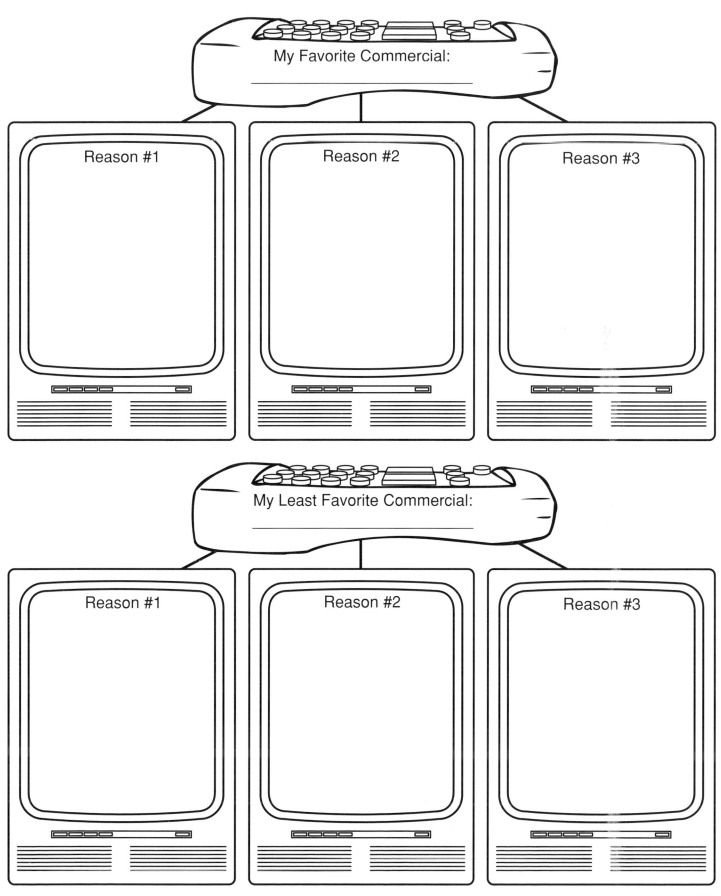

My Favorite Commercial:

_____

| Reason #1 | Reason #2 | Reason #3 |

My Least Favorite Commercial:

_____

| Reason #1 | Reason #2 | Reason #3 |

My Best Friend

PROMPT

Imagine that your best friend is feeling down. A good way to encourage someone is by telling the person why you appreciate him or her. In a clarification paragraph, identify your best friend and name some of the qualities that make that person special.

Think It!

1. There are many books, poems, and movies whose theme is friendship. Ask volunteers to name some examples and to think about why friendship is so important. Lead them to focus specifically on how friendship is important in their lives.

2. Explain to your students that in clarification writing the writer states whether he likes or dislikes something. Further explain that the writer then supports his reasoning with three or more details and summarizes his opinion in a concluding sentence.

3. Read aloud the prompt above, display it on a transparency, or write it on the board. Then give each student one copy of page 27.

4. Direct each student to use the reproducible to help organize his thoughts about the qualities of his best friend.

Write It!

1. Have each student use the information recorded on page 27 to help write a clarification paragraph about his best friend on another sheet of paper. Instruct the student to name the person he likes, explain why he or she is his best friend with three or more specific details, and summarize his paragraph with a concluding sentence.

2. Direct the student to proofread and edit his work carefully. Encourage students to swap papers to peer-edit. After all corrections have been made, have each student write his final copy on another sheet of paper.

3. If desired, make copies of the students' paragraphs. Have the students take home their original paragraphs in order to mail or give them to their best friends. Then have the students bring in photos of their best friends. Post each student's picture and copied paragraph onto a bulletin board titled "My Best Friend."

Name _____

My Best Friend

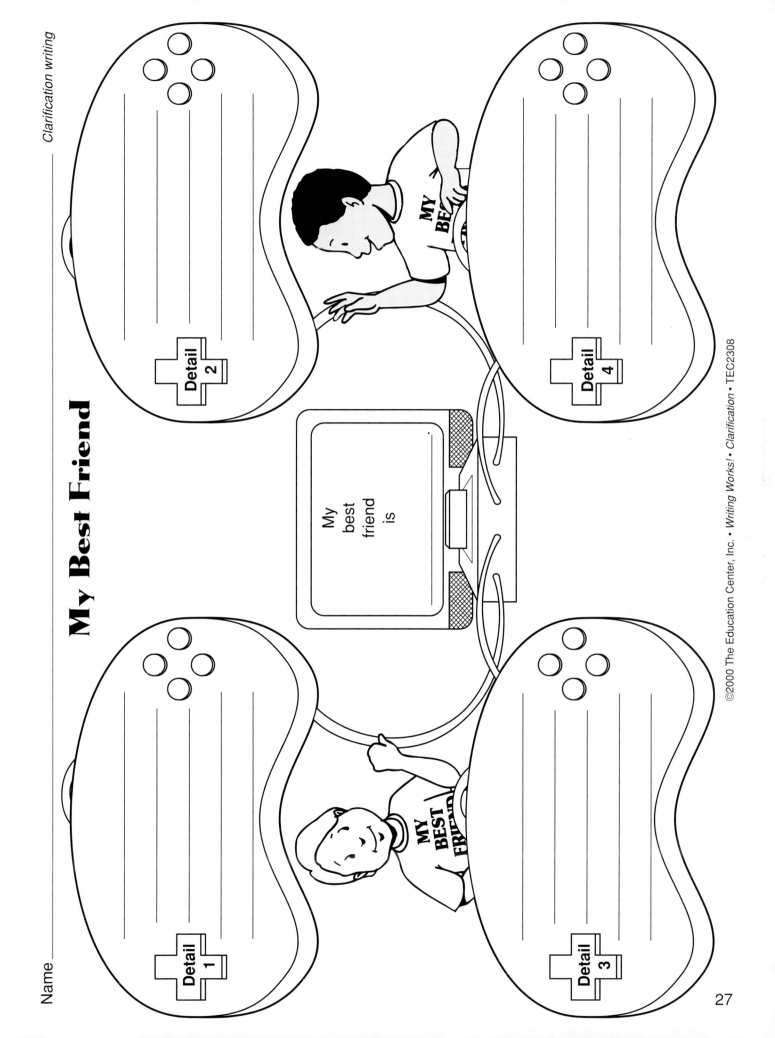

Detail 1

Detail 2

Detail 3

Detail 4

My best friend is

Our Favorite Authors

Who is your favorite author? What book(s) did that person write that you enjoy? Why do you like this author's stories? Write a clarification paragraph about your favorite author.

Think It!

1. Brainstorm with your students a list of favorite authors and the books that these authors have written. Have several student volunteers share with the class why these books are so good.

2. Explain to your students that in clarification writing, the writer states whether she likes or dislikes something and supports the statement with three or more details. Then she summarizes her opinion in a concluding sentence.

3. Read aloud the prompt above, display it on a transparency, or write it on the board. Then give each student one copy of page 29.

4. Direct each student to use page 29 to help her organize her thoughts about why her chosen author is her favorite and why his or her books are so good. In the space provided, have her write the name of the author and then complete the rest of the page to explain her choice.

Write It!

1. Have each student use the information recorded on page 29 to help write a clarification paragraph about her favorite author on another sheet of paper. Instruct the student to state the author she likes, explain her choice with three or more specific details, and summarize her paragraph with a concluding sentence.

2. Direct the student to proofread and edit her work carefully. Encourage students to swap papers to peer-edit. After all corrections have been made, have the student write her final copy on another sheet of paper.

3. If desired, make a class book out of the students' paragraphs and place it on your class bookshelf. Temporarily fill the bookshelf only with books by the authors represented in the students' clarification paragraphs. Title the bookshelf "Our Favorite Authors."

Our Favorite Authors

Choose your favorite author.

List the book(s) that you've read by this author.

_____   _____

_____   _____

Check off the items below that describe this author's book(s).

<table>
<tr><td>☐ Great characters</td><td>☐ Happy</td></tr>
<tr><td>☐ Interesting plots</td><td>☐ Sad</td></tr>
<tr><td>☐ Good settings</td><td>☐ Serious</td></tr>
<tr><td>☐ Funny</td><td>☐ Relates to your life</td></tr>
<tr><td>☐ Exciting</td><td>☐ Teaches you something</td></tr>
<tr><td>☐ Scary</td><td>☐ Other ideas: _____</td></tr>
<tr><td>☐ Adventurous</td><td>_____</td></tr>
</table>

Pick the three best descriptions of this author's work and give specific examples from his or her book(s). Use the back of this sheet if necessary.

1 _____   2 _____   3 _____

_____   _____   _____

_____   _____   _____

_____   _____   _____

Our Town

A person who has never been to your town or city would like to know the best and the worst things about it. In two clarification paragraphs, tell the one thing you like most and the one thing you dislike most about your community.

Think It!

1. Get students thinking about their town or city. Gather pictures and facts about the community from the local newspaper and library and share the information with your class. Then ask class members to discuss how their town or city might appear to a newcomer or visitor. Record their observations on the board.

2. Explain to your students that in clarification writing the writer states whether he likes or dislikes something and supports the statement with three or more details. Then he summarizes his opinion in a concluding sentence.

3. Read aloud the prompt above, display it on a transparency, or write it on the board. Then give each student one copy of page 31.

4. Direct each student to use the reproducible to help organize his thoughts about the qualities of his town or city.

Write It!

1. Have each student use the information recorded on page 31 to help write two clarification paragraphs about his town or city on another sheet of paper. Instruct the student to state the one thing he likes most at the beginning of the first paragraph and the thing he dislikes most at the beginning of the second paragraph. Next, have him support each opinion with three or more specific details and summarize each paragraph with a concluding statement.

2. Direct the student to proofread and edit his work carefully. Encourage students to swap papers to peer-edit. After all corrections have been made, have the student write his final copy on another sheet of paper.

3. If desired, display a map of your town or city in the center of a bulletin board titled "Our Town." As each student finishes his paragraphs, have him write what he likes on one index card and what he dislikes on another index card, with his name on each. Then post the likes to the left of the map and the dislikes to the right of the map. Also, keep the students' paragraphs near the display so that others can discover why a classmate did or did not like a particular feature of his town or city.

Our Town

I like _

Supporting Details

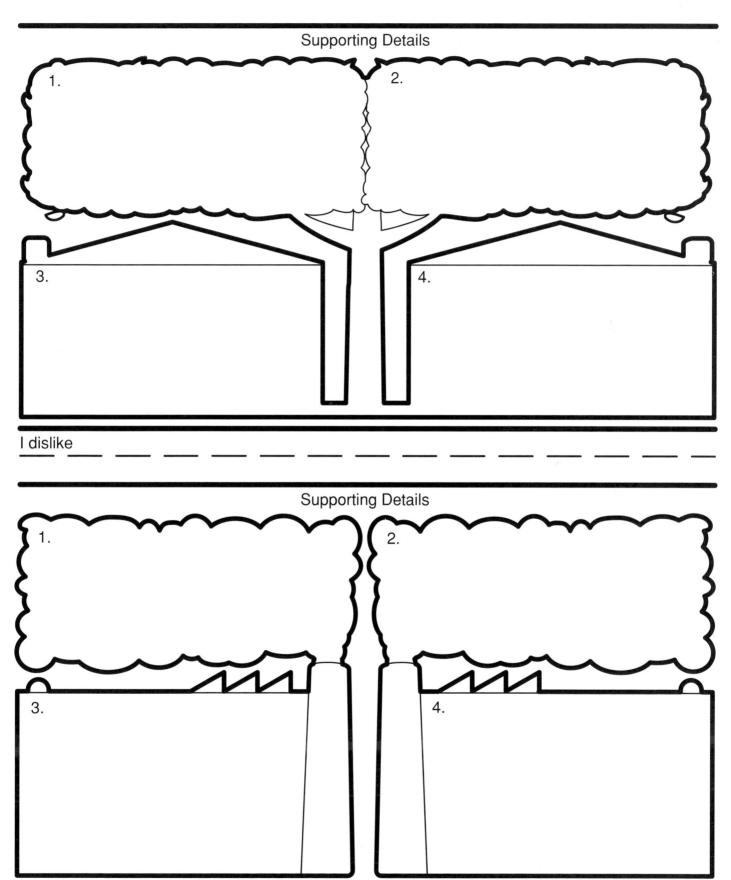

1.

2.

3.

4.

I dislike _ _ _ _ _ _ _ _ _ _ _ _ _ _ _ _ _ _

Supporting Details

1.

2.

3.

4.

Interesting Insects or Creepy-Crawlies?

PROMPT *Think about all the different types of insects in the world. Which ones do you think are interesting and which ones do you think are creepy? In two clarification paragraphs explain why you like one insect and why you dislike another insect.*

Think It!

1. Share this riddle with students: I have three body parts and an exoskeleton. I sense my surroundings using short hairs on my antennae, feet, or mouthparts. There are more of my kind than any other animal on the planet. I can be helpful to humans, but I can also be very harmful. Who am I? *(an insect)* Ask student volunteers to share why they think some people like insects and why others dislike them.

2. Explain to your students that in clarification writing, the writer states whether she likes or dislikes something. Further explain that the writer then supports her reasoning with three or more details and summarizes her opinion in a concluding sentence.

3. Read aloud the prompt above, display it on a transparency, or write it on the board. Then give each student a copy of page 33.

4. Direct each student to use page 33 to help her organize her thoughts for each paragraph.

Write It!

1. Have the student use the information recorded on page 33 to help write two clarification paragraphs about the insect she likes and the insect she dislikes on another sheet of paper. Remind the student to include in each paragraph a topic sentence that states her opinion, at least three detail sentences that explain her reasoning, and a concluding sentence.

2. Direct the student to proofread and edit her work carefully. Encourage students to swap papers to peer-edit. After all corrections have been made, have the student write her final copy on another sheet of paper.

3. If desired, use the following idea to showcase your students' work. Draw a large ladybug pattern, make a class supply, and give one to each student. Direct the student to cut out the pattern, color the front of the ladybug, and glue her final copy onto the back, trimming away excess paper. Staple all of the ladybugs together to make a class book. Make a front and back cover for the book by tracing one of the ladybug patterns twice onto a sheet of tagboard. Color and cut out each pattern and staple to the front and back of the book accordingly. Title the book "Interesting Insects or Creepy-Crawlies?"

Interesting Insects or Creepy-Crawlies?

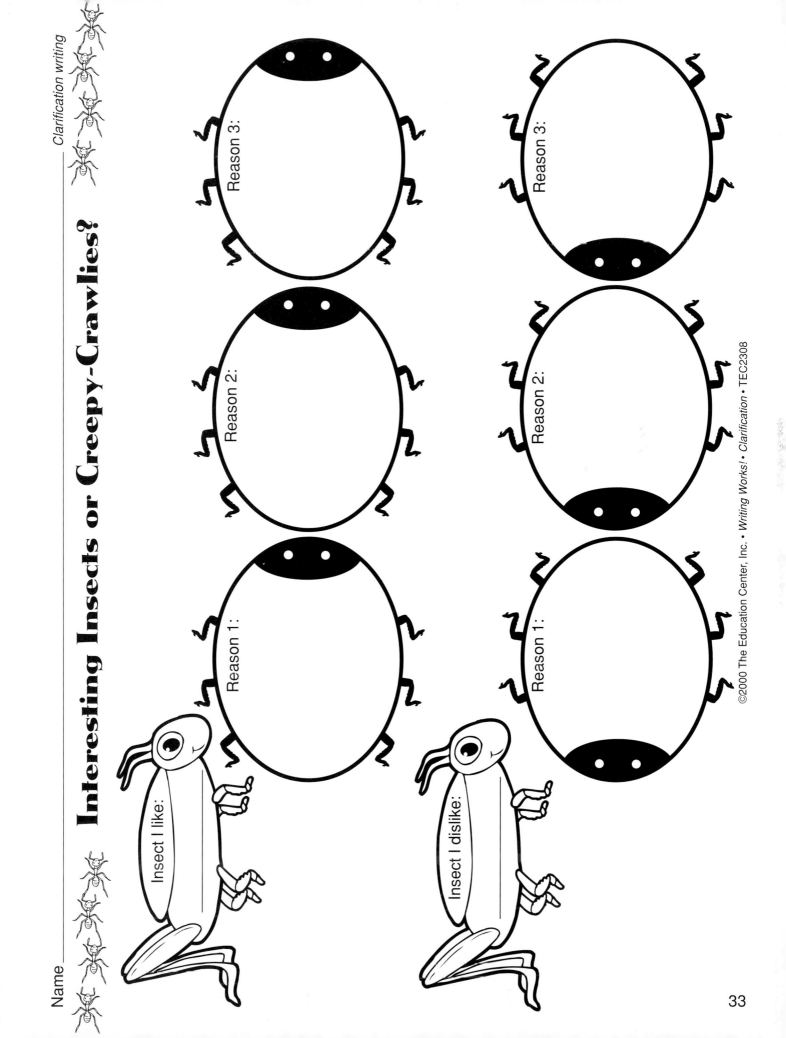

Insect I like: _____

Reason 1:

Reason 2:

Reason 3:

Insect I dislike: _____

Reason 1:

Reason 2:

Reason 3:

Delicious Dining

PROMPT

Your family is taking you to your favorite restaurant for your birthday. In two clarification paragraphs, explain why you like your favorite restaurant and why you dislike your least favorite restaurant.

Think It!

1. Share with students your favorite and least favorite types of restaurants and the reasons why they are your favorite and least favorite. Then brainstorm with students different types of restaurants, such as Chinese, Italian, or steak. List student responses on the board. Ask student volunteers to share their favorite and least favorite types of restaurants and why they are their favorites and least favorites.

2. Explain to your students that in clarification writing the writer states whether he likes or dislikes something. Further explain that the writer then supports his reasoning with three or more details and summarizes his opinion in a concluding sentence.

3. Read aloud the prompt above, display it on a transparency, or write it on the board. Then give each student a copy of page 35.

4. Direct the student to use page 35 to help organize his thoughts for each paragraph.

Write It!

1. Have each student use the information recorded on page 35 to help him write, on another sheet of paper, two clarification paragraphs about his favorite and least favorite types of restaurants. Remind the student to include in each paragraph a topic sentence that states his opinion, at least three detail sentences that explain his reasoning, and a concluding sentence.

2. Direct the student to proofread and edit his work carefully. Encourage students to swap papers to peer-edit. After all corrections have been made, have the student write his final copy on another sheet of paper.

3. If desired, use the following idea to display your students' work. Give each student a paper plate. Direct the student to glue his final copy onto the plate. Cover a bulletin board with a red checkered tablecloth, and display the students' plates on the board. Title the board "Delicious Dining."

Delicious Dining

My favorite restaurant is _____.

Reason 1	Reason 2	Reason 3

My least favorite restaurant is _____.

Reason 1	Reason 2	Reason 3

One Special Person

PROMPT *Think about all the people who are important to you and who have played a special part in your life. Pick one of these people to write about. Then write a clarification paragraph about this person, explaining why he or she is so special to you.*

Think It!

1. Tell your students a story about a person who meant a great deal to you when you were their age. Then have students think of special people in their lives and brainstorm a list of some of their characteristics. Write their responses on the board.

2. Explain to your students that in clarification writing, the writer states whether she likes or dislikes something and supports the statement with three or more details. Then she summarizes her opinion in a concluding sentence.

3. Read aloud the prompt above, display it on a transparency, or write it on the board. Then give each student one copy of page 37.

4. Direct each student to use the reproducible to help her organize her thoughts about her special person. Tell her to write her own name in the appropriate space at the bottom of the page. Then have her draw a picture of her special person and write his or her name in the banner under the picture she's drawn.

Write It!

1. Have each student use the information recorded on page 37 to help write a clarification paragraph about the person she's chosen on another sheet of paper. Instruct the student to state who that person is, explain her choice with three or more specific details, and summarize her paragraph with a concluding sentence.

2. Direct the student to proofread and edit her work carefully. Encourage students to swap papers to peer-edit. After all corrections have been made, have the student write her final copy on another sheet of paper.

3. If desired, have students cut out the bottom portion of their reproducibles; then mount them onto a bulletin board titled "One Special Person." Display each student's paragraph below her cutout. Turn this project into an event by having the students invite their special people to class for readings of the paragraphs and refreshments.

One Special Person

Conclusion: _____

Meet one of the
special people
in my life.

By _____

School Vogue

In some schools, children wear uniforms so that everyone has the same color or style of clothing. In a clarification paragraph, tell whether you would like to wear a uniform to school.

Think It!

1. Divide the class into groups of five or six members. Write the following question on the board: "Why do you think some schools require students to wear uniforms?" Allow groups time to discuss the question and record their responses. Then have a student report his group's responses to the class. Write their answers on the board.

2. Explain to your students that in clarification writing, the writer states whether he likes or dislikes something and supports the statement with three or more details. Then he summarizes his opinion in a concluding sentence.

3. Read aloud the prompt above, display it on a transparency, or write it on the board. Then give each student one copy of page 39.

4. Direct each student to use the reproducible to help him organize his thoughts about whether he likes or dislikes the idea of school uniforms.

Write It!

1. Have each student use the information recorded on page 39 to help write, on another sheet of paper, a clarification paragraph about whether students should or should not wear uniforms. Instruct the student to share the option he favors, support it with three or more specific details, and summarize his paragraph with a concluding statement.

2. Direct the student to proofread and edit his work carefully. Encourage students to swap papers to peer-edit. After all corrections have been made, have the student write his final copy on another sheet of paper.

3. If desired, bind students' paragraphs into a class "fashion magazine." For the cover of your magazine, fold a 12" x 18" piece of construction paper in half. Then create a collage on your cover. Have each student cut out one picture from a fashion magazine or catalog and glue the picture to the front or back of the cover, leaving space for the title. Title the magazine "School Vogue: Wearing School Uniforms" and place it in the reading center for students to enjoy.

School Vogue

Opinion/Topic Sentence:

Supporting Details:

1

2

3

4

Conclusion: _____

Musical Fan or Critic?

There are many different types of music. Which type is your favorite? Which is your least favorite? In two clarification paragraphs, explain why you like your favorite type of music and why you dislike your least favorite type of music.

Think It!

1. Before teaching this lesson, gather several selections of different types of music, such as jazz, classical, reggae, rap, country, and rock 'n' roll.

2. With your students, share the music selections you gathered. Ask student volunteers to share their favorite and least favorite types of music.

3. Explain to your students that in clarification writing, the writer states whether she likes or dislikes something. Further explain that the writer then supports her reasoning with three or more details and summarizes her opinion in a concluding sentence.

4. Read aloud the prompt above, display it on a transparency, or write it on the board. Then give each student a copy of page 41.

5. Direct each student to use page 41 to help organize her thoughts for each paragraph.

Write It!

1. Have each student use the information recorded on page 41 to help her write, on another sheet of paper, two clarification paragraphs about her favorite and least favorite types of music. Remind the student to include a topic sentence that states her opinion, at least three detail sentences that explain her reasoning, and a concluding sentence in each paragraph.

2. Direct the student to proofread and edit her work carefully. Encourage students to swap papers to peer-edit. After all corrections have been made, have the student write her final copy on another sheet of paper.

3. If desired, have a class concert. Ask students to bring samples of their favorite types of music and a snack. After students have shared their paragraphs, invite them to listen to the music and enjoy their snacks!

Musical Fan or Critic?

My Favorite Type of Music: _____

Reason 1

Reason 2

Reason 3

My Least Favorite Type of Music: _____

Reason 1

Reason 2

Reason 3

Movie Reviews

PROMPT

Movie reviewers rate movies using stars. Think about a movie you would rate five stars (the best) and a movie you would rate one star (the worst). In two clarification paragraphs, explain why you would give one movie five stars and the other movie one star.

Think It!

1. Using the movie review section of a local newspaper or magazine, discuss appropriate movie reviews with the class. Then ask student volunteers to rate a movie they've seen on a scale of one to five stars, with five stars being the highest and one star being the lowest.

2. Explain to your students that in clarification writing, the writer states whether he likes or dislikes something. Further explain that the writer then supports his reasoning with three or more details and summarizes his opinion in a concluding sentence.

3. Read aloud the prompt above, display it on a transparency, or write it on the board. Then give each student a copy of page 43.

4. Direct the student to state the movie he would rate five stars and the movie he would rate one star and his reasons for each on page 43.

Write It!

1. Have each student use the information recorded on page 43 to help him write on another sheet of paper two clarification paragraphs about the movie he rated five stars and the movie he rated one star. Remind the student to include a topic sentence that states his opinion, at least three detail sentences that explain his reasoning, and a concluding sentence in each paragraph.

2. Direct the student to proofread and edit his work carefully. Encourage students to swap papers to peer-edit. After all corrections have been made, have the student write his final copy on another sheet of paper.

3. If desired, staple students' final copies onto several large sheets of newsprint. Staple the paper together to create a class newspaper titled "Movie Reviews."

Movie Reviews

Five-Star Movie

☆ ☆ ☆ ☆ ☆   ☆ ☆ ☆ ☆ ☆

_____

Reason 1: _____

_____

_____

Reason 2: _____

_____

_____

Reason 3: _____

_____

_____

One-Star Movie

☆   ☆

_____

Reason 1: _____

_____

_____

Reason 2: _____

_____

_____

Reason 3: _____

_____

_____

Proofreading Checklist

To the Student: Use this checklist during the proofreading or editing stage of your writing to help you determine what needs improving and/or correcting before writing the final version. Then give this checklist and your writing to a peer editor (a classmate) to use to edit your work.

Title of Writing Selection:_____

Things to Check	Writer's Checklist		Peer Editor's Checklist	
	Yes	No	Yes	No
1. Does the writing make sense and is it easy to read?				
2. Does each paragraph contain a topic sentence?				
3. Does the writing contain three or more supporting details and/or reasons?				
4. Do all the details/reasons stick to the topic?				
5. Does each paragraph contain a concluding sentence?				
6. Did the writer use descriptive words?				
7. Does each sentence begin with a capital letter?				
8. Does each sentence have an ending punctuation mark?				
9. Did the writer use complete sentences?				
10. Did the writer check for misspelled words?				
11. Is each paragraph indented?				

☆ If the peer editor checked "No" in any box above, discuss it with the editor.

Think About It!

I think I did a _____ job on this writing selection because…

_____

_____

Clarification-Writing Assessment

Student's Name: _____ **Date:** _____

Title of Writing: _____

Assessment Items	Agree	Disagree
1. The writing selection makes sense; it is easy to read.		
2. Each paragraph contains a topic sentence.		
3. The writing selection contains three or more supporting details and/or reasons.		
4. All details relate to the topic.		
5. Details and/or reasons are presented in a logical order.		
6. Each paragraph contains a concluding sentence.		
7. Each paragraph is indented.		
8. Correct punctuation is used.		
9. Each sentence begins with a capital letter.		
10. Each word is spelled correctly.		
11. Run-on sentences and incomplete sentences are avoided.		
12. Each verb agrees with its subject.		
13. All proper nouns are capitalized.		
14. Descriptive words are used.		
15. Apostrophes are correctly used to form contractions and to show possession.		

Comments: _____

_____

_____

_____

Extra Prompts

1. Imagine that you are at a restaurant and you can have any dessert you want. Think about your favorite and least favorite desserts. In two clarification paragraphs, explain why you like your favorite dessert and why you dislike your least favorite dessert.

2. Saturday and Sunday make up the weekend. In one clarification paragraph, explain what you like about the weekend.

3. Everyone has to shop for items such as food, clothing, or household supplies. What is your favorite and what is your least favorite thing about shopping? In two clarification paragraphs, explain what you like about shopping and what you dislike about shopping.

4. Imagine that you are going on a trip with your family. Think about your favorite place to go. In one clarification paragraph, explain what you like about your favorite place.

5. Think about lunchtime at your school. What do you like and what do you dislike about it? In two clarification paragraphs, explain what you like about lunchtime and what you dislike about lunchtime.

6. An important rule in life is to share with others. For example, you may have been asked to share your toys at home or your paper at school. In two clarification paragraphs, explain what you like about sharing and what you dislike about sharing.

7. Think about your bedroom. What is your favorite part of your room? What is your least favorite part? In two clarification paragraphs, explain why you like your favorite part and why you dislike your least favorite part.

8. Think about some of the games you have played with your friends. What is your favorite game and what is your least favorite game? In two clarification paragraphs, explain what you like about your favorite game and what you dislike about your least favorite game.

Extra Prompts

9. Think about the different ways a person can get exercise, such as running, playing sports, or bicycling. What is your favorite way to get exercise and what is your least favorite? In two clarification paragraphs, explain what you like about your favorite way to get exercise and what you dislike about your least favorite way to get exercise.

10. Some people like to be scared, such as when watching a scary movie or reading a scary book. Do you like being scared? In one clarification paragraph, explain why you like or dislike being scared.

11. When you write, do you like to use a pen or a pencil? In two clarification paragraphs, explain what you like about using either the pen or the pencil and what you dislike about using either the pen or the pencil.

12. Everyone has a bedtime. Do you think your bedtime is fair or unfair? In one clarification paragraph, explain why you think your bedtime is either fair or unfair.

13. Think about all of the different hats people wear, such as baseball hats, ski hats, straw hats, and cowboy hats. What is your favorite type of hat to wear? In one clarification paragraph, explain what you like about your favorite type of hat.

14. Think about your name. What do you like about your name? In one clarification paragraph, explain what you like about your name.

15. There are hundreds of kinds of candy. Think about your favorite candy and your least favorite candy. In two clarification paragraphs, explain what you like about your favorite candy and what you dislike about your least favorite candy.

16. There are many different sports on TV. Think about your favorite sport to watch and your least favorite sport to watch. In two clarification paragraphs, explain what you like about your favorite sport and what you dislike about your least favorite sport.

Editing Symbols

Writers use special marks called *editing symbols* to help them edit and revise their work. Editing symbols are used to show what changes a writer wants to make in his or her writing.

Symbol	Meaning	Example
◯	Correct spelling.	(animl)
ℯ	Delete or remove.	dogg
◡	Close the gap.	fi sh
∧	Add a letter or word.	lives in tree a
#	Make a space.	flies south
⌐＿	Reverse the order of a letter, a word, or words.	plants eats
⋀	Insert a comma.	the crab an arthropod
⊙	Insert a period.	Cats purr
⋎	Insert an apostrophe.	a deers antlers
⋓ ⋓	Insert quotation marks.	She said, Look at the pig.
≡	Make the letter a capital.	birds eat seeds.
/	Make the letter lowercase.	a Snowshoe hare
¶	Start a new paragraph.	¶Some dogs have tails.